The
Oxford Picture Dictionary
for the
CONTENT AREAS

Carolyn Graham

Reproducibles

Content Chants

OXFORD
UNIVERSITY PRESS

Oxford University Press
198 Madison Avenue
New York, NY 10016 USA

Great Clarendon Street
Oxford OX2 6DP England

Oxford New York
Auckland Bangkok Buenos Aires Cape Town Chennai
Dar es Salaam Delhi Hong Kong Istanbul Karachi Kolkata
Kuala Lumpur Madrid Melbourne Mexico City Mumbai Nairobi
São Paulo Shanghai Taipei Tokyo Toronto

OXFORD is a trademark of Oxford University Press.

The Oxford Picture Dictionary for the Content Areas Reproducibles: Content Chants
ISBN 0-19-434886-5

Editorial Manager: Shelagh Speers
Editors: Marilyn Rosenthal, Paul Phillips, June Schwartz
Associate Production Editor: Peter Graham
Elementary Design Manager: Doris Chen Pinzon
Designer: Nona Reuter
Art Buyer: Stacy Godlesky
Production Manager: Abram Hall

Printing (last digit): 10 9 8 7 6 5 4 3 2 1

Printed in Hong Kong.

Illustrations by Mary Chandler.

Cover design by Nona Reuter and Doris Chen Pinzon.

Oxford University Press is a department of the University of Oxford. It furthers the University's objective of excellence in research, scholarship, and education by publishing worldwide.

The
Oxford Picture Dictionary
for the
CONTENT AREAS

Content Chants

The Oxford Picture Dictionary for the Content Areas Content Chants contains photocopiable versions of the 60 *Content Chants* that accompany the topics of the *Dictionary*. The playful and humorous *Content Chants* in this collection provide fun speaking, listening, and reading practice for each topic's content and vocabulary.

Recordings of the *Content Chants* are available on *The Oxford Picture Dictionary for the Content Areas Cassettes/CDs.*

Further ideas and instructions on using the *Content Chants* are found throughout *The Oxford Picture Dictionary for the Content Areas Teacher's Book.*

The Oxford Picture Dictionary for the Content Areas Program

The Oxford Picture Dictionary for the Content Areas is a vocabulary development program designed for elementary and middle school students who are learning English. The *Dictionary* presents over 1,500 words drawn from the content areas of social studies, history, science, and math. The words are presented in full page illustrations that place the words in context. Each illustration introduces a content-related topic. The 60 topics are organized into eight units. Each topic generally has from 12 to 22 numbered vocabulary items which are also illustrated.

The *Dictionary* can be used with the following components to make it suitable for an English language curriculum:

The *Teacher's Book* presents strategies and techniques for presenting, practicing and expanding the vocabulary and language in each of the 60 topics. Each topic includes an annotated list of current and classic books to help teachers create a classroom library.

The *Reproducibles Collection* is a boxed set of four books of reproducible pages that contains the following components:

- The *Word and Picture Cards* feature black and white photocopiable versions of the words and their illustrations from the *Dictionary*.

- The *Content Readings* explain each topic as it is depicted in the *Dictionary* while incorporating the content words and language structures.

- The *Content Chants* provide vocabulary reinforcement and further practice in language and content through rhythmic chants.

- The *Worksheets* offer additional practice of the language structures and content presented in each topic.

The four books in the *Reproducibles Collection* are also available separately.

The *Workbook* provides written practice and reinforcement of the vocabulary presented in each *Dictionary* topic.

The *Wall Charts* are full-color poster-size reproductions of the 60 topic pages from the *Dictionary*.

The *Cassettes/CDs* contain all the words in the *Dictionary* as well as the *Content Reading* and *Content Chants*, all recorded in clear, natural speech.

The *Dictionary* is available in both monolingual and bilingual editions.

CLASSROOM CHANT

Computer, * overhead projector,
pens, pencils, books, and crayons.
Computer, * overhead projector,
pencil sharpener, bulletin board.

Is this your classroom?
Yes, it is.

Are these your books?
Yes, they are.

Is this your pen?
Yes, it is.

Are these your crayons?
Yes, they are.

Pens, pencils, books, and crayons.
Pencil sharpener, bulletin board.

Is there a computer in the classroom?
Yes, there is.

Is there a cassette player?
Yes, there is.

Is there an overhead projector?
Yes, there is.

Wow! You have everything!

Computer, * overhead projector,
pens, pencils, books, and crayons.
Computer, * overhead projector,
pencil sharpener, bulletin board.

WHERE'S THE COACH?

Where's the coach?
He's not in the gym.

There he is!

That's not him!
That's the custodian. That's not him.

Where's the coach?
He's not in the gym.

Here he comes!

That's not him!
That's the librarian. That's not him.

Look on the playground.
There! With Tim.

That's not the coach. That's not him.
He's not on the playground. That's not him.

Where's the coach? He's not in the gym.

THERE'S A HOUSE

There's a house. * There's a big, white house.
There's a bathroom in the house,
    In the big white house.
There's a sink in the bathroom,
    In the big white house.

There's a boy at the sink in the bathroom in
the house.
He's washing his hands,
    In the big white house,
At the sink, in the bathroom,
    In the big white house.

There's a bedroom in the house,
    In the big white house.
There's a bed in the bedroom,
    In the big white house.

There's a girl in the bed in the bedroom in
the house.
She's taking a nap,
    In the big white house,
In the bed, in the bedroom,
    In the big white house.

Oxford Picture Dictionary for the Content Areas, Content Chants by Carolyn Graham

Topic 3 / **The House**

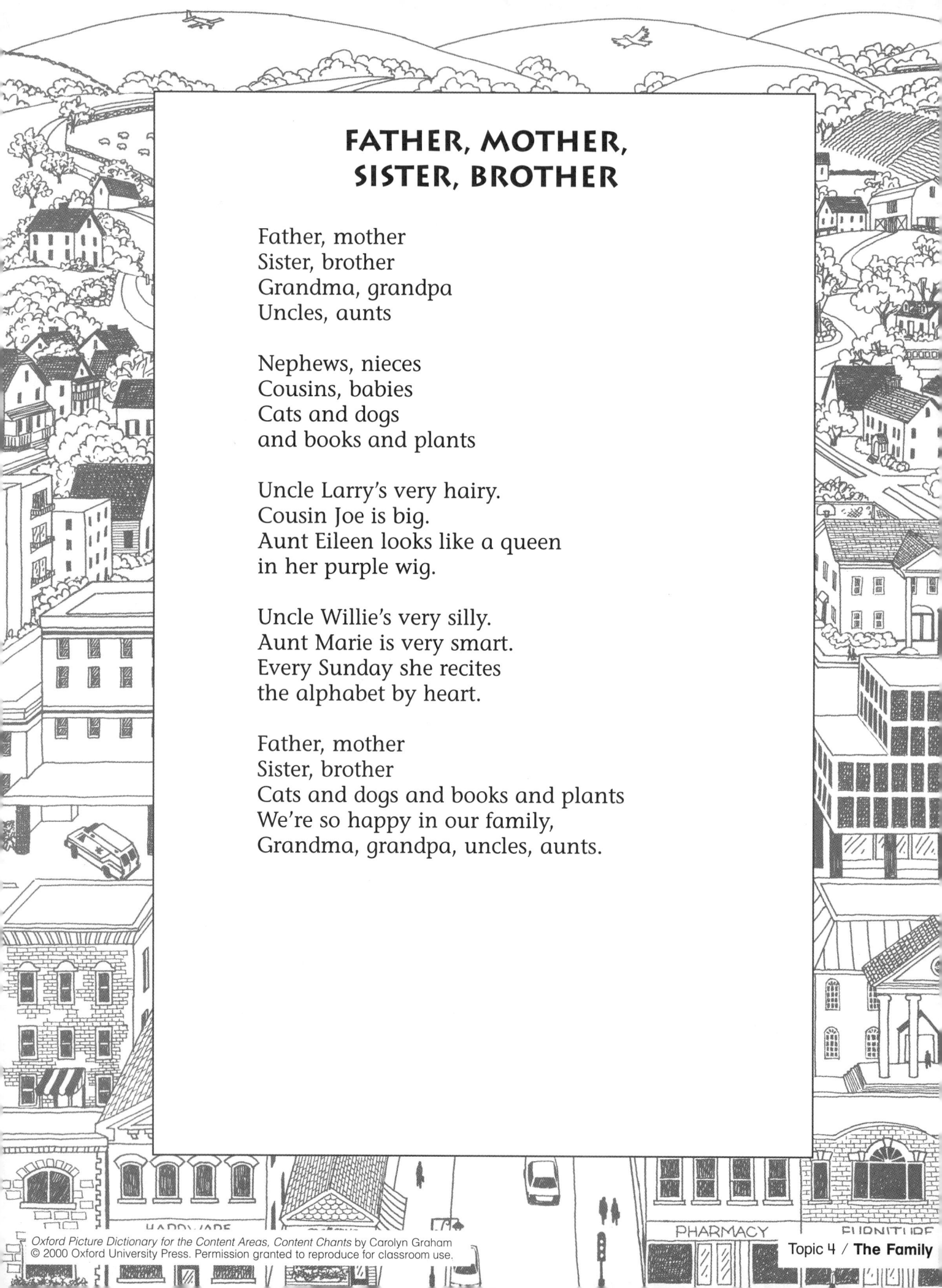

FATHER, MOTHER, SISTER, BROTHER

Father, mother
Sister, brother
Grandma, grandpa
Uncles, aunts

Nephews, nieces
Cousins, babies
Cats and dogs
and books and plants

Uncle Larry's very hairy.
Cousin Joe is big.
Aunt Eileen looks like a queen
in her purple wig.

Uncle Willie's very silly.
Aunt Marie is very smart.
Every Sunday she recites
the alphabet by heart.

Father, mother
Sister, brother
Cats and dogs and books and plants
We're so happy in our family,
Grandma, grandpa, uncles, aunts.

I LIKE THE CITY

I like the city.
    I do, too.
    There's so much to see,
    so much to do.

Look at the buildings
touching the sky.
I love the city.
    So do I.

    I like department stores.
So do I.
There's so much to look at,
so much to buy.

If you love the city,
follow me.
Summer or winter,
that's the place to be.

Yellow taxis,
Neon light.
My favorite city
is up all night.

WALK ON THE SIDEWALK

Walk on the sidewalk,
not on the street.
Swim in the swimming pool. *

Stop at the stoplight.
Cross at the crosswalk.
Swim in the swimming pool. *

Drive in the driveway,
not on the sidewalk.
Swim in the swimming pool. *

Ride your bike,
but not on the sidewalk.
Swim in the swimming pool. *

Cross at the crosswalk.
Stop at the stoplight.
Swim in the swimming pool. *

Oxford Picture Dictionary for the Content Areas, Content Chants by Carolyn Graham
© 2000 Oxford University Press. Permission granted to reproduce for classroom use.

I LIKE THE COUNTRY

I like the country.

So do I.

I like the white clouds
in the bright blue sky,
the big red barns,
and the cows going moo,
and the little red rooster going
cock-a-doodle-doo.

I love the country.
I really do.
I like the green hills,
and the orchards, too.
The ponds and the pastures,
the woods and the streams.
I see the country
in my dreams.

Oxford Picture Dictionary for the Content Areas, Content Chants by Carolyn Graham
© 2000 Oxford University Press. Permission granted to reproduce for classroom use.

KENNY'S ON CRUTCHES

Kenny's on crutches.
Cathy's in a cast.
Willie's in a wheelchair,
moving fast.

Sally's on a stretcher.
Bobby's in a bed.
The nurse has a blanket
and a pillow for his head.

Andy's in an ambulance.
So is Pete.
They were driving too fast
on a busy street.

Mommy had a baby.
I'm as happy as can be.
Now I've got a little brother
and he looks like me.

SHE'S A CARPENTER

She's a carpenter.
She makes things.

He's a construction worker.
He builds things.

She's a salesperson.
She sells things.

He's a messenger.
He delivers things.

She's a mechanic.
She fixes things.

He's a plumber.
He fixes sinks.

She's a hairdresser.
She fixes hair.

He's a dentist.
He fixes teeth.

Oxford Picture Dictionary for the Content Areas, Content Chants by Carolyn Graham
© 2000 Oxford University Press. Permission granted to reproduce for classroom use.

RIDDLE CHANT

There are fifty states in the U.S.A.,
fifty states from sea to sea.
There are four states that start with A,
but not one state that starts with B.

There are three states that start with C.
There is one state that starts with D.
Which are the states that start with C?
Which is the state that starts with D?

There are two states that start with S.
There are two states that start with T.
Can you name the states that start with S?
Can you name the states that start with T?

There are fifty states in the U.S.A.,
plus Washington D.C.
Fifty states in the U.S.A.,
but none of them starts with B.

BUY THE NEWSPAPER

Buy the newspaper.
Look at the headlines.
Turn on the radio.
Listen to the news.

Look at the headlines.
Read the newspaper.
Turn on the television.
Listen to the news.

Turn on the television.
Listen to the newscaster.
Watch the stock market.
Listen to the news.

Watch the stock market.
Listen to the newscaster.
　　Buy? Sell?
　　What should I do?

Read the newspaper.
Listen to the radio.
Turn on the television.
Watch the news!

THE SOUTH

The South *
    Alabama
The South *
    Mississippi
The South *
    Louisiana

Cotton, rice, and sugarcane

The South *
    Georgia peaches
The South *
    Florida oranges
The South *
    Louisiana catfish

Cotton, rice, and sugarcane

The South *
    raw materials
The South *
    factory workers
The South *
    assembly lines

Cotton, rice, and sugarcane

Oxford Picture Dictionary for the Content Areas, Content Chants by Carolyn Graham
© 2000 Oxford University Press. Permission granted to reproduce for classroom use.

PLOW THE FIELD, PLANT THE CORN

Plow the field.
Plant the corn.
Harvest the corn.
Feed America.

Corn muffins
Cornbread
Cornflakes
Corn on the cob

Plow the field.
Plant the wheat.
Harvest the wheat.
Feed America.

Whole wheat bread
Whole wheat bagels
Whole wheat muffins
Whole wheat cereal

Corn on the cob,
Whole wheat bread.
Feed America.
Feed the world!

COWBOY, COW

Cowboy, cow, buffalo, buffalo
Cowboy, cow, buffalo herd
Cowboy, cow, buffalo, buffalo
Buffalo grazing, near the corral.

Look at the cowboy on his horse.
Look at the cowboy near the corral.
Look at the cowboy, look at the cows.
Look at the buffalo near the corral.

Cowgirl, cow, buffalo, buffalo
Cowgirl, cow, buffalo herd
Cowgirl, cow, buffalo, buffalo
Buffalo grazing, near the corral.

Look at the cowgirl on her horse.
Look at the cowgirl near the corral.
Look at the cowgirl, look at the cows.
Look at the buffalo near the corral.

Oxford Picture Dictionary for the Content Areas, Content Chants by Carolyn Graham
© 2000 Oxford University Press. Permission granted to reproduce for classroom use.

REDWOOD FOREST

Redwood forest
Tall trees
Strong trees
Old trees

Strong lumberjacks
pick up a chain saw,
cut down the trees,
redwood trees.

Strong lumberjacks
cut down the trees,
take them to the sawmill,
turn them into lumber.

Strong lumberjacks
Strong trees
Redwood forest
Tall trees

Puget Sound, full of fish.
Young fishermen in their boats
throw their nets in the cold water.
Catch the fish, fresh fish!

Cannery workers clean the fish.
Cannery workers cut the fish.
Cannery workers put them into cans.
Canned fish, canned fish!

Oxford Picture Dictionary for the Content Areas, Content Chants by Carolyn Graham
© 2000 Oxford University Press. Permission granted to reproduce for classroom use.

HOW TO GET RICH IN TEXAS

Go to Texas.
Buy a drill.
Take your drill and
dig a well.

Dig a well
and find oil.
Pump that oil out. *

Pump that oil, ship that oil.
Send it through the pipeline.
Send it through the pipeline.

Send it through the pipeline
or store it in a tank.
Put your money in a great big bank.

Drill for oil.
It's not hard.
I found some
in my backyard.

Drill for oil.
It's not hard.
You might find some
in your backyard.

SAN FRANCISCO, CALIFORNIA

San Francisco, California.
Tourists riding cable cars.
Climbing hills in San Francisco.
Golden Gate Bridge, Wow!

San Jose, California.
Microchips, fiber optics.
Lots of cars in California.
Freeways and shopping malls.

Hollywood, California.
Lots of actors out of work.
Actresses, waiting on tables.
Lots of actors working out.

Hawaii, lots of tourists.
Spending money here and there.
Hawaii, Pacific Ocean.
Surfing, swimming everywhere.

CANADA AND MEXICO

Canada is north of the U.S.A.
Canadians come here every day.
They come to work. They come to play.
Canadians come here every day.
Americans go there every day.
They go to work. They go to play.

Mexico is south of the U.S.A.
Mexicans come here every day.
They come to visit. They come to stay.
Mexicans come here every day.
Americans go there every day.
They go to visit. They go to stay.

Canada is cold.
Mexico's not.
Canada is chilly.
Mexico is hot.

Canada has polar bears.
Mexico does not,
'cause Canada's cold
and Mexico's hot.

BOW AND ARROW

Bow and arrow.
Hunt the deer.
Shoot the deer.
Kill the deer.

Take the hide.
Dry it in the sun.
Wear the deerskin.
Thank the deer.

Take the hide.
Make a tepee.
Wear the deerskin.
Thank the deer.

Gather nuts.
Grind the corn.
Kill the buffalo.
Kill the deer.

Eat the meat.
Wear the hide.
Thank the buffalo.
Thank the deer.

COLUMBUS SAILED
ACROSS THE SEA

Columbus sailed
across the sea
without a phone,
without TV.

No fax, no e-mail, no PC
when Columbus sailed
across the sea.

When he woke up
in the middle of the night,
the moon and stars
were his only light.

Without an engine,
only a sail,
it wasn't easy,
but he didn't fail.

The crew was fine.
The masts were strong.
On his three little ships,
The journey was long.

Columbus sailed
into history
without a phone,
without TV.

We give Columbus
the highest score,
though he didn't find
what he was looking for.

Oxford Picture Dictionary for the Content Areas, Content Chants by Carolyn Graham
© 2000 Oxford University Press. Permission granted to reproduce for classroom use.

LIGHT THE CANDLES,
LISTEN TO THE BELLS

Light the candles.
Listen to the bells.

Light the candles.
Look at the cross.

Light the candles.
Listen to the bells.
Look at the cross
on top of the church.

Walk through the patio.
Stop at the fountain.
Listen to the fountain.
Listen to the bells.

Light the candles.
Listen to the bells.
Look at the cross
on top of the church.

Oxford Picture Dictionary for the Content Areas, Content Chants by Carolyn Graham
© 2000 Oxford University Press. Permission granted to reproduce for classroom use.

TOWN MEETING

Town meeting, meetinghouse,
courthouse, inn *

Town meeting, meetinghouse,
courthouse, inn *

The Pilgrims are meeting.
    Where are they meeting?
They're meeting in the meetinghouse,
next to the inn.

    Where's the inn?
It's next to the courthouse.
    Where's the courthouse?
It's next to the inn.

Town meeting, meetinghouse,
courthouse, inn *

Town meeting, meetinghouse,
courthouse, inn *

CANNONBALL, CANNON

Cannonball, cannon,
Continental soldier

Redcoat, minuteman,
bayonet. Hey!

Load the rifle.
Shoot the rifle.
Fire the cannonball.
Light up the sky!

Cannonball, cannon,
Continental soldier

Musket, powder horn
bayonet. Hey!

Pick up the powder horn.
Load the musket.
Shoot the musket.
Light up the sky!

PRINTER, PRINTING PRESS

Printer, printing press
Pamphlet, quill
Start the printing press.

    * I will.

Printer, printing press
Pamphlet, quill
Read the pamphlet.

    * I will.

Look at the signature.
    Thomas Jefferson

Look at the signature.
    Benjamin Franklin

Look at the signatures.
    John Hancock
    John Adams

    * We're free!
No more kings, no more queens.
Good–bye George the Third.
We're free!

No more kings, no more queens.
Good–bye George the Third.
We're free!

PIONEERS, PACKING UP

Pioneers
packing up,
moving west,
following a dream.

How did they come?

They came by water:
flatboat,
steamboat,
raft, canoe.

How did they come?

They came by land:
stagecoach,
wagon train,
covered wagon.

Pioneers,
they came by land.
Pioneers,
they came by sea.
Pioneers,
moving west.
Pioneers,
following a dream.

Oxford Picture Dictionary for the Content Areas, Content Chants by Carolyn Graham
© 2000 Oxford University Press. Permission granted to reproduce for classroom use.

CALIFORNIA GOLD

Sail on a clipper ship.
Ride on a mule.
Go to California.
Look for gold.

Go to California,
Northern California.
Pick up a shovel.
Dig for gold.

Go to California.
Walk to a stream.
Pick up a pan.
Pan for gold.

Sail on a clipper ship.
Ride on a mule.
Go to California.
Look for gold!

CIVIL WAR,
A NATION DIVIDED

Civil War,
a nation divided.
North against South,
Civil War.

Yankees against Rebels,
blue against grey.
Brother fought brother,
Civil War.

Who won the war?
  The North won the war.

Who lost the war?
  The South lost the war.

Mothers lost sons,
sisters lost brothers,
children lost fathers,
in the Civil War.

  "A house divided
  Against itself,"
A nation divided
by the Civil War.

Oxford Picture Dictionary for the Content Areas, Content Chants by Carolyn Graham
© 2000 Oxford University Press. Permission granted to reproduce for classroom use.

DON'T FORGET TO VOTE

Senate *
House of Representatives
Congress *
Legislative branch

Senate *
House of Representatives
Congress *
Don't forget to vote.

Here comes the President.
Stand up!
Executive branch
Oval Office

Here comes the President.
Stand up!
Don't forget to vote.
Don't forget to vote.

Judicial branch
Supreme Court
Nine judges, here they come!
Count them, count them one by one.
Nine judges, here they come!

Senate *
House of Representatives
Congress *
Legislative branch

Senate *
House of Representatives
Congress *
Don't forget to vote.

HUMAN RIGHTS

Human rights
Equal rights

Women's rights
The right to vote

    Susan B. Anthony
    Equal rights
    Women's rights
    The right to vote

Farm workers' rights
Fair pay

    Cesar Chavez
    Farm workers' rights

Black and White
Equal rights

    Martin Luther King
    Civil rights

Who helped the women?
    Susan B. Anthony

Who helped the African Americans?
    Martin Luther King

Who helped the farm workers?
    Cesar Chavez

Equal rights
Human rights

HIS FEET ARE BIG

His feet are big.
His legs are long.
His arms are strong.
He's a basketball player. * *

Her waist is small.
Her neck is long.
Her toes are strong.
She's a dancer. * * *

His legs are short.
His arms aren't long.
His ankles, knees, and back are strong.
He's a jockey. * * *

Her eyes are good.
Her arms are strong.
Her body is thin. Her legs are long.
She's a tennis player. * *

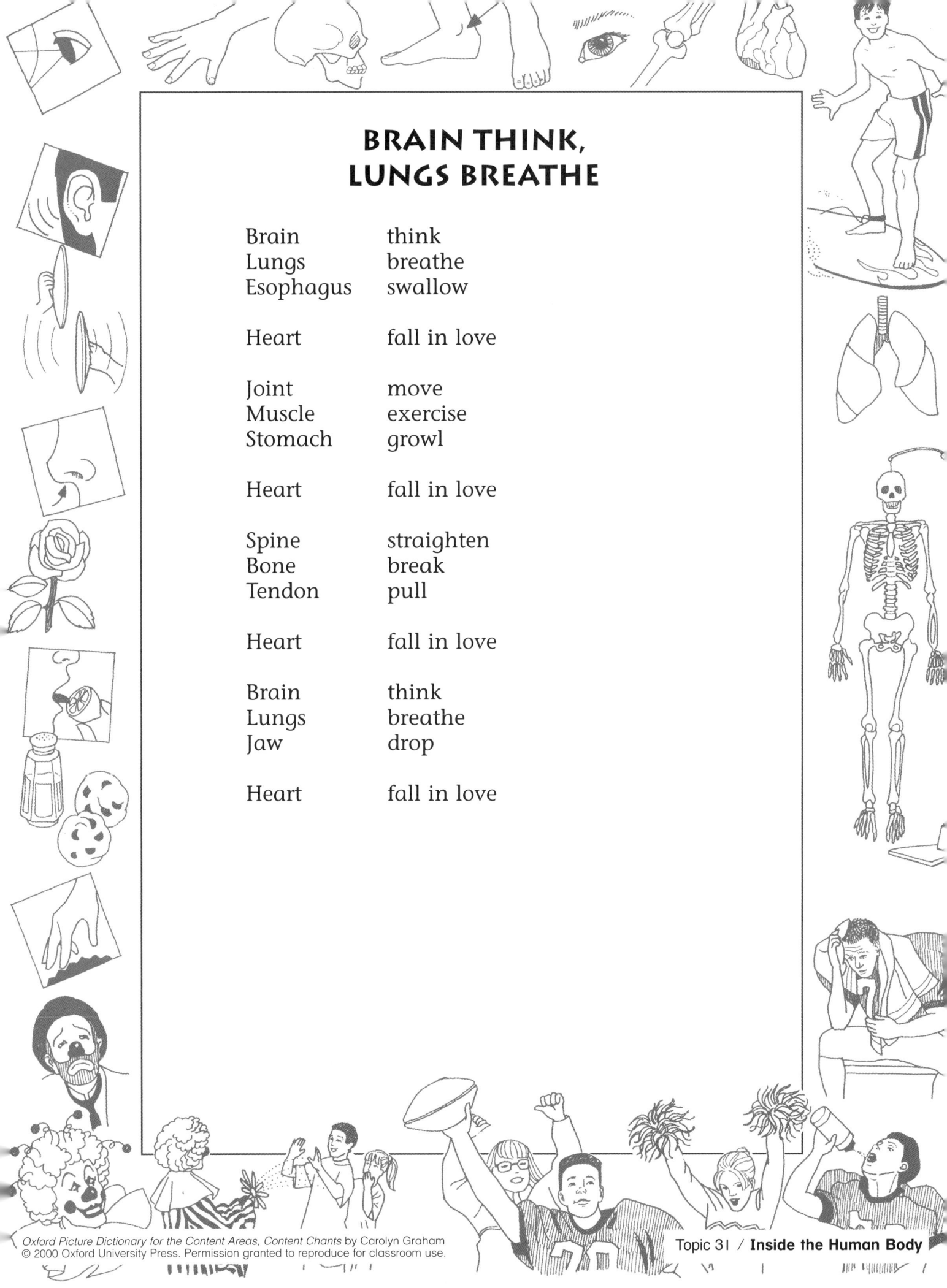

BRAIN THINK,
LUNGS BREATHE

Brain	think
Lungs	breathe
Esophagus	swallow
Heart	fall in love
Joint	move
Muscle	exercise
Stomach	growl
Heart	fall in love
Spine	straighten
Bone	break
Tendon	pull
Heart	fall in love
Brain	think
Lungs	breathe
Jaw	drop
Heart	fall in love

THE SENSES CHANT

Touch *
    smooth, rough

Don't touch the stove. It's hot! *

Taste *
    sweet, sour, salty

Taste the soup! It's wonderful.

See *
    bright, dark

Turn on the lights. I can't see a thing.

Hear *
    loud, soft

Speak up! * I can't hear you.

Smell *
    fragrant, foul

What's that smell?
    Phew!

FEELINGS

I'm excited. *
We're winning. * *

I'm proud. *
We won! * *

I'm scared. *
We're losing. * *

I'm sad. *
They won! * *

He's angry. *
They lost. * *

She's surprised. *
We won! * *

They're sad. *
We're happy. *
We're proud. *
We won! * *

PUT ON YOUR SAFETY GLASSES

Put on your safety glasses.
Pick up the tweezers.
Pick up a leaf.
Put it on the slide.
Look at it under the microscope.
Now turn it over.
Eeeeeeeek! Look at the little bug!

Observe, * classify,
measure very carefully.
Observe, * classify,
study the data.
Fill out the chart.

Observe, * classify,
measure very carefully.
Start a collection.
Start it today.
      Where's the little bug?
He ran away.

PROTISTS HAVE ONE CELL, NOT TWO

Protists have one cell, not two.
You can't see them. They can't see you.

Monerans * are very small.
You can't see monerans at all.
But you better be careful, you better take care,
'cause monerans * are everywhere!

"I'm a vertebrate," *
said the dog to the frog.
"Well, so am I," said the frog to the dog.
"Not me," said the octopus,
"no, not me,
but I'm just fine at the bottom of the sea."

PLANT CHANT

Plant a bulb.
Watch it grow.
Strong roots
Long stem
Green leaves
Beautiful flowers
Soft petals
Tiger lily

Plant a seed.
Watch it grow.
Little pine tree, young branches
Little leaves, little needles
Young pine tree
Watch it grow.

Old pine tree
Strong trunk
Strong limbs
Brown bark
Green needles
Brown pinecones
Beautiful pine tree
Watch it grow.

MUSHROOM, BROCCOLI

Mushroom, broccoli,
cauliflower pie.
She hates broccoli.
     So do I.

String beans, celery,
cauliflower stew.
He hates broccoli.
     So will you.

Onions, lima beans,
yams. Hooray!
They eat broccoli every day.

I ate broccoli
in my dream.
I love broccoli * ice cream!

PLEASE HAVE AN APPLE!

Please have an apple!
They're right over there.

    I don't want an apple.
    I want a pear.
    I don't want an apple,
    not today.

"An apple a day
keeps the doctor away."

    I don't care.
    I want a pear.

How about a peach?

    I don't want a peach.

How about strawberries? They're OK.

    But I ate all the strawberries yesterday!

Oxford Picture Dictionary for the Content Areas, Content Chants by Carolyn Graham
© 2000 Oxford University Press. Permission granted to reproduce for classroom use.

FLATWORMS ARE FLAT

Flatworms are flat.
They're not round.
You won't find one
on the ground.
They like water,
ponds, and streams.
You might see one
in your dreams.

Flatworms are flat,
but that's OK.
I like flatworms anyway.

Roundworms are round,
but they're not fat.
Roundworms are round
and that is that!

DO YOU LIKE CLAMS?

Do you like clams?

> Yes, I do.

> I like clams and oysters, too.

Do you eat squid?

> Yes, I do.

> I eat squid and octopus, too.

Do you cook crayfish?

> Yes, I do.

> I cook crayfish and lobster, too.

How about shrimp?

> They're not for me.

> I like shrimp, but they don't like me.

Oxford Picture Dictionary for the Content Areas, Content Chants by Carolyn Graham
© 2000 Oxford University Press. Permission granted to reproduce for classroom use.

ANTS WALK

Ants walk,
grasshoppers jump,
butterflies fly,
but caterpillars crawl.

Mosquitoes bite,
bees sting,
crickets chirp,
but caterpillars crawl.

Ants walk,
grasshoppers jump,
spiders bite,
but caterpillars crawl.

Spiders bite,
crickets chirp,
butterflies fly,
but caterpillars crawl.

SWORDFISH, CATFISH

Swordfish, catfish
tuna fish, shark
Don't go swimming
in the ocean, in the dark.

If you meet a shark
in the middle of the sea,
treat him very
carefully.

Bluefish, goldfish
pipefish, cod
I think catfish
are very odd.

I've never seen one
in the sea,
so I don't know
what they think of me.

Oxford Picture Dictionary for the Content Areas, Content Chants by Carolyn Graham
© 2000 Oxford University Press. Permission granted to reproduce for classroom use.

TADPOLES SWIM, RATTLESNAKES BITE

Tadpoles swim.
Rattlesnakes bite.
Crocodiles crawl around all night.

Garter snakes move very fast.
Turtles usually come in last.

Chameleons love to sit around,
changing color from green to brown.

Salamanders swim.
Iguanas chew.
They have four legs.
You have two.

Oxford Picture Dictionary for the Content Areas, Content Chants by Carolyn Graham
© 2000 Oxford University Press. Permission granted to reproduce for classroom use.

PENGUINS CAN'T FLY

Penguins can't fly.
Neither can I.
Eagles do.
Pigeons do, too.

A duck can swim,
but so can you.
Crows are noisy.
Seagulls are, too.

Parrots talk.
Hummingbirds sing.
Peacocks show off
everything.

Oxford Picture Dictionary for the Content Areas, Content Chants by Carolyn Graham
© 2000 Oxford University Press. Permission granted to reproduce for classroom use.

DOGS ARE BIGGER
THAN PUPPIES

Dogs are bigger than puppies.
Lambs are smaller than sheep.
Horses are not at all like cats.
They stand up when they sleep.

Little pigs are piglets.
A foal is a baby horse.
A little cat is a kitten.
His dad is a cat, of course.

Bunnies hop.
Rabbits run.
Cows stand around
in the sun.

Dogs are bigger than piglets.
Horses are smarter than sheep.
Cats are not at all like cows.
They curl up when they sleep.

TIGER, ELEPHANT, KANGAROO

Tiger, elephant,
kangaroo.
Wild animals in the zoo.
You like them, but they don't like you.
Tiger, elephant,
kangaroo.

Watch the monkeys.
Look at the lion.
Talk to the zebra in the zoo.

But don't pet the lion.
Don't touch the tiger.
You'll be sorry if you do!

Tiger, elephant,
kangaroo.
Wild animals in the zoo.
You like them, but they don't like you.
Tiger, elephant,
kangaroo.

DIPLODOCUS WAS
VERY STRONG

Diplodocus was very strong.
Diplodocus was ninety feet long.
His teeth were sharp, his neck was strong.
Diplodocus was very long.

Brachiosaurus was very tall.
His tail was long, his head was small.
Brachiosaurus was easy to see.
When he got hungry, he'd eat a tree.

Triceratops was strange to see,
with horns on his head: one, two, three.
He didn't look at all like you or me.
Triceratops was strange to see!

Stegosaurus was a frightening sight.
With spikes on his tail, he was up all night,
munching on plants, munching on trees.
Stegosaurus was easy to please.

Tyrannosaurus Rex was the dinosaur king.
He could do almost anything.
When he got hungry and wanted more,
he'd eat another dinosaur.

POLLUTION CHANT

Smog, smoke,
Air pollution.
Smoke, smokestack,
Air pollution.
Cars, trucks,
Air pollution.
     Pollution. *
     What's the solution?

Exhaust, *
Air pollution.
Oil slick,
Water pollution.
Landfill,
Soil pollution.
     Pollution. *
     What's the solution?

Carpools. *
That's a solution.
Recycling. *
That's a solution.
Don't litter. *
That's a solution.
     Pollution. *
     We're the solution!

WATER FREEZES, ICE MELTS

Water freezes.
Ice melts.
Water evaporates.
Water boils.

Water freezes.
Water into ice.
Ice melts.
Physical changes.

Water boils.
Water into steam.
Physical changes.
Physical changes.

Flour and water,
pounded into dough,
baked into bread.
Chemical changes.

Flour and sugar,
chocolate chips,
baked into cookies.
Chemical changes.

HEAT, LIGHT, SOUND

Heat, light, sound *
Heat, light, sound *
Feel the heat.
Feel the sun.
See the light.
Look at the sunrise.
Hear the sound.
Listen to the thunder.
Listen to the thunder roll. *

Push it. *
Pull it. *
Put it on wheels.
Put it on wheels.

Push it. *
Pull it. *
Put it on wheels.
Put it on wheels.

Axle *
Pulley *
Put it on wheels.
Put it on wheels.

Push it. Pull it.
Put it on wheels.
Look at it go!
Wow!

LOOK AT THE MOON

Look at the Moon.
Look at the stars.
Is that Jupiter?
Or is that Mars?

Is that a planet?
Or a very bright star?
You can't see Neptune.
It's too far.

Venus rising
is a glorious sight.
And lots of constellations
will be out tonight.

ISLAND, OCEAN, RIVER, VALLEY

Island, ocean, river, valley
Mountain, * volcano *

Island, ocean, river, valley
Mountain, * volcano *

Sail to the island.
Dive in the ocean.
Fish in the river.
Walk in the valley.

Sail to the island.
Climb the mountain.
See the volcano.
Walk on the lava bed.

Sail to the island.
Dive in the ocean.
Fish in the river.
Walk in the valley.

Climb the mountain.
See the volcano.
Walk on the lava bed.
Wow!

IT'S GREAT TO LIVE
IN THE POLAR ZONES

It's great to live in the polar zones,
if you're a penguin or a polar bear.
It's great to live in the polar zones,
though I wouldn't want to live there.

It's tough to live in the tundra.
I don't know what I'd do
if I had a house in the tundra
with all those caribou.

It's fun to live in the tropical zone
with monkeys in the trees.
You won't need a sweater, scarf, or gloves.
Your hands will never freeze.

The grassland's great, if you like grass.
The desert's fine, if you love sand.
The taiga's OK if you're a bear.
If not, it might not be so grand.

But it's great to live in the polar zones,
if you're a penquin or a polar bear.
It's great to live in the polar zones,
though I wouldn't want to live there.

WILL IT RAIN TODAY?

Will it rain today?
Or will it snow?
Don't listen to the forecaster.
He doesn't know.
When he says,
"We won't have wind or rain,"
we'll probably get a hurricane.

He promised us sunshine,
and what did we get?
We got very, very wet!

Oxford Picture Dictionary for the Content Areas, Content Chants by Carolyn Graham
© 2000 Oxford University Press. Permission granted to reproduce for classroom use.

EVEN NUMBERS, ODD NUMBERS

Even numbers
    2, 4
Odd numbers
    1, 3
Even numbers
    2, 4, 6, 8, 10 *
Even numbers
    2, 4
Odd numbers
    1, 3
Odd numbers
    1, 3, 5, 7, 9 *

Add, subtract, and multiply.
Add, subtract, and multiply.
Add *
    2 plus 2.
    2 plus 2 is 4. *
Subtract *
    4 minus 2.
    4 minus 2 is 2. *
Multiply *
    4 times 2.
    4 times 2 is 8. *
Add, subtract, and multiply.
Add, subtract, and multiply.

GEOMETRY CHANT

Plane figure
octagon
Plane figure
square *

How many sides in an octagon?
How many sides in a square? *

Plane figure
octagon
Plane figure
square *

Eight sides in an octagon
Four sides in a square *

How many sides in an octagon?
Eight sides
Stop sign

How many sides in a pentagon?
Five sides
Cross-walk sign

Solid figure, cylinder
Plane figure, square

Cylinder, garbage can
Plane figure, square *

RIGHT ANGLE,
STRAIGHT ANGLE

Right angle
Straight angle
Intersecting lines

Compass
Diameter
Intersecting lines

Circumference
Symmetrical
Intersecting lines

Compass
Diameter
Intersecting lines

Height, width, length *
Intersecting lines

Height, width, length *
Intersecting lines

How high is it?
    It's very high.
How long is it?
    It's very long.
How wide is it?
    It's very wide.

Intersecting lines *

SIXTEEN OUNCES, ONE POUND

Sixteen ounces
  One pound
Two thousand pounds
  One ton

How many pounds?
  Two thousand pounds.

Hey! *
That's heavy! *

Two pints of milk
  One quart
Four quarts of milk
  One gallon

How much milk?
  One gallon.

My, my! *
That's a lot of milk!

ASCENDING ORDER, GOING UP

Ascending order
Going up
Gaining weight
Getting taller

Descending order
Coming down
Losing weight
Getting smaller

Look at the chart.
Study the chart.
Ken's getting taller every day.

Look at the table.
Study the table.
Anna's getting thinner every day.

PC CHANT

Cursor, keyboard
monitor, mouse
There's a personal computer
in my house.

Diskette, disk drive
Where's the CD?
My personal computer
is looking for me.

Cursor, keyboard
monitor, mouse
I like that PC
in my house.

It's user-friendly
if you try,
but don't forget to switch on
the power supply.